W9-CIM-608

EMMA WATSON

Kathleen Tracy

Mitchell Lane
PUBLISHERS

P.O. Box 196
Hockessin, Delaware 19707
Visit us on the web: www.mitchelllane.com
Comments? email us: mitchelllane@mitchelllane.com

Printing   1   2   3   4   5   6   7   8   9

A Robbie Reader
Contemporary Biography

Abigail Breslin	Albert Pujols	Alex Rodriguez
Aly and AJ	Amanda Bynes	AnnaSophia Robb
Ashley Tisdale	Brenda Song	Brittany Murphy
Charles Schulz	Dakota Fanning	Dale Earnhardt Jr.
David Archuleta	Demi Lovato	Donovan McNabb
Drake Bell & Josh Peck	Dr. Seuss	Dwayne "The Rock" Johnson
Dylan & Cole Sprouse	Eli Manning	Emily Osment
Emma Watson	Hilary Duff	Jaden Smith
Jamie Lynn Spears	Jennette McCurdy	Jesse McCartney
Jimmie Johnson	Johnny Gruelle	Jonas Brothers
Jordin Sparks	Justin Bieber	Keke Palmer
Larry Fitzgerald	LeBron James	Mia Hamm
Miley Cyrus	Miranda Cosgrove	Raven-Symoné
Selena Gomez	Shaquille O'Neal	Story of Harley-Davidson
Syd Hoff	Taylor Lautner	Tiki Barber
Tom Brady	Tony Hawk	Victoria Justice

Library of Congress Cataloging-in-Publication Data
Tracy, Kathleen.
  Emma Watson / by Kathleen Tracy.
     p. cm. — (A Robbie reader)
  Includes filmography.
  Includes bibliographical references and index.
  ISBN 978-1-58415-901-8 (library bound)
  1. Watson, Emma, 1990– —Juvenile literature. 2. Actors—Great Britain—
Biography—Juvenile literature. I. Title.
  PN2598.W25T73 2010
  791.4302'8092—dc22
  [B]

                                                              2010014897

ABOUT THE AUTHOR: Kathleen Tracy has been a journalist for over twenty years. Her writing has been featured in magazines including *The Toronto Star*'s "Star Week," *A&E Biography* magazine, *KidScreen*, and *TV Times*. She is also the author of over 85 books, including numerous books for Mitchell Lane Publishers, such as *The Fall of the Berlin Wall*; *Paul Cézanne*; *The Story of September 11, 2001*; *The Clinton View*; *We Visit Cuba*; *Mariah Carey*; and *Kelly Clarkson*. Tracy lives in the Los Angeles area with her two dogs and African Grey parrot.

PUBLISHER'S NOTE: The following story has been thoroughly researched and to the best of our knowledge represents a true story. While every possible effort has been made to ensure accuracy, the publisher will not assume liability for damages caused by inaccuracies in the data, and makes no warranty on the accuracy of the information contained herein. This story has not been authorized or endorsed by Emma Watson.

TABLE OF CONTENTS

Words in **bold** type can be found in the glossary.

Emma Watson is famous for her role of Hermione Granger in the Harry Potter films. Rupert Grint plays Ron Weasley. Hermione and Ron are Harry's two best friends.

The Kiss

Emma Watson was very nervous. She had to film her first onscreen kiss in *Harry Potter and the Deathly Hallows*—and not with just anybody. It was going to be with her costar Rupert Grint, who plays Ron Weasley. Talk about awkward!

"I'm trying not to think about it," Emma admitted beforehand to *The Sydney Morning Herald*.

When the day finally arrived, Rupert and Emma were still uncomfortable.

"We weren't looking forward to it really," she recalled to *Entertainment Daily*. "It was a horrible thing to have to do because we are just like brother and sister. We were both just like, Oh my . . . I can't believe we have to do this!"

Emma says when the scene started, "I was so desperate to get it over with, I pounced on him. After the first take he was like, 'Whoa, there! Where did that come from?'" She laughed.

They had to reshoot the scene four more times—because Emma and Rupert couldn't stop giggling. "We were both determined to get it right the first time," Rupert told *The Daily Mail* newspaper, "but our first try was a disaster. We both felt so **self-conscious** [self-KON-shus], we couldn't stop laughing."

"We just couldn't take it seriously," Emma agreed.

To her and Rupert's relief, they finally got it right. "We have watched the playback and it's good," she said.

Emma was twenty years old when she finished filming *The Deathly Hallows*, which would be shown in two parts. She had spent over half her life making Harry Potter movies.

Emma provided the voice of Princess Pea in the 2008 film *The Tale of Despereaux*. At the Los Angeles premiere, Emma got a kiss on the hand from a life-sized Despereaux.

And it all started because her dad would read to her before she went to bed.

When Emma and her brother Alex were young, they lived in France. After their parents divorced, they moved to Oxford, England, with their mother, Jacqueline.

Dream Come True

Emma Charlotte Duerre Watson was born in
Paris, France, on April 15, 1990. Her bother
Alex was born three years later.

Emma's parents, Jacqueline Luesby and
Chris Watson, are both attorneys (uh-TUR-
nees). When Emma was five, Jacqueline and
Chris divorced. Emma and Alex moved to
Oxford, England, with their mother. Emma still
visits Paris regularly to see her **maternal** (muh-
TER-nal) grandmother (her mother's mother).
"I really love it. It feels a bit like home," she said
in *The Sydney Morning Herald*.

Even as a toddler, Emma enjoyed performing in front of an audience. When she was seven years old, she won a poetry **competition** (kom-peh-TIH-shun). She took classes at a local theater school and studied singing, dancing, and acting.

At eight years old, Emma started attending the Dragon School. Despite its name, students there do not learn about dragons and wizardry. It is a **boarding school** named after an old story called *St. George and the Dragon*.

A year after she entered, casting agents showed up at her school. Casting agents hire people to star in movies or on TV series. In this case, they were casting for the first Harry Potter movie. Emma was thrilled! She loved the Harry Potter books.

"My dad used to read them to me before I went to bed and while on long car journeys," she explained in *Interview* magazine. The casting agents selected twenty students, including Emma. "They took my photograph in the school gym, and then I got a call three weeks later."

Emma's favorite Harry Potter book is *Harry Potter and the Prisoner of Azkaban*. She never imagined she would become friends with Potter author J.K. Rowling, pictured above.

Emma says she and Hermione are alike in that they are both independent. Although Hermione is a **muggle**, over time she becomes a powerful witch and frequently helps Harry fight evil.

Emma **auditioned** (aw-DIH-shund) eight different times. "I just felt like that part belonged to me. I know that sounds crazy, but from that first audition, I always knew."

She was determined to win the role of Hermione (her-MY-uh-nee) Granger. That worried Emma's parents. They didn't want her to be disappointed if she didn't get the part.

One night, after her dad roasted a chicken, he gave Emma the wishbone. "I obviously made the wish that I would get this role," she told *Interview*.

And she did. Out of thousands of girls, Emma was going to play Hermione in *Harry Potter and the Sorcerer's Stone*.

What happened to the wishbone? "I still have that wishbone upstairs in my jewelry box," Emma admitted to *Interview*.

Wishbone

One of Emma's favorite hobbies is dancing. She has taken classes for modern, breakdance, body-popping, and street dance.

Rise to Fame

Emma couldn't believe she was going to be in a movie. Neither could her friends and schoolmates.

"My friends were all amazed," she told *The Sunday Mirror.* "They knew I was auditioning but I hadn't told them too much about it. I thought that if I did it would jinx it."

When she told her friends she got the part, they didn't believe her. "I had to say, 'I really have got the part, ask my mum, I'm not fooling around with you, this is real.'" Even so, Emma guessed that many of her friends wouldn't believe her until the movie came out.

Emma admitted she was nervous, but she says the adult actors were extremely nice to her, Rupert, and Daniel Radcliffe. She says she wouldn't have been able to come to the set if she hadn't felt completely safe.

She admitted to *The Sydney Morning Herald* that she gave Hermione many of her own traits. "We're both feminists, we're both very stubborn, both very determined and quite loyal," she said. "If I have a friend, then I

Though the Harry Potter films are over, Emma remains close with Rupert Grint and Daniel Radcliffe. The three costars got to make handprints at Grauman's Chinese Theatre in Hollywood.

stay through to the end." She's also geeky like Hermione, too. "We both love school. I love to learn."

As expected, *Harry Potter and the Sorcerer's Stone* was a huge hit. Suddenly, Emma was famous. At home with either parent, her life did not change. Her mother and father still expected her to follow the rules and help with the chores. "It doesn't matter what's going on in my life, I get the same treatment from my parents," Emma said in *Girls' Life*.

But the rest of her life changed a lot. Suddenly, people recognized her walking down the street. And starting with the second Harry Potter movie, Emma spent at least eight months of the year filming. The sound stage where they worked became known as Potterworld. And for the next ten years, it became Emma's second home.

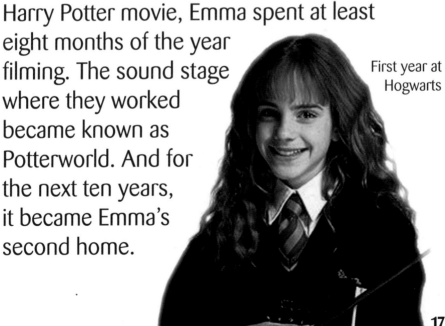

First year at Hogwarts

17

Emma, Daniel, and Rupert were ten, eleven, and twelve years old when the first Harry Potter movie, *Harry Potter and the Sorcerer's Stone*, was released.

Growing Up in Potterworld

Like Hermione, Emma is an **overachiever** (oh-ver-uh-CHEE-ver). In 2003 she graduated from the Dragon School and went to the all-girls Headington School. When she wasn't filming a Harry Potter movie, she attended regular classes at Headington. "It took a while for people to realize that . . . I'm normal," she told *Interview* about her treatment there. "I didn't get bullied or pushed against lockers or anything."

Emma just wanted to fit in and be like everyone else. "I don't want any special treatment," she told *Girls' Life*. "I don't want to be made a fuss of."

Emma said in *Interview* that her friends take her fame in stride and "don't even think about it. If I get recognized, they'll laugh and say, 'Oh, yeah, I forgot—you're famous.'"

Even when that happens, she told *Girls' Life* that she still doesn't feel famous. "I forget that I am, and someone will stop me on the street and I'll remember. So it is weird. It's not important to me. I don't need people to know my name."

In addition to being an A student, Emma was active in sports. She played tennis, golf, and rounders, which is the British version of baseball. She also participated in track, running hurdles and the 100-meter dash. She was best at field hockey.

"I'm really competitive," she admitted in *CosmoGirl*. "Field hockey is my strongest sport, and if I lose a game, I take a long, hot bath and moan about it."

What is her biggest sport dream? To play **Quidditch** (KWIH-ditch). "Oh . . . I wish!" she told *Interview*.

Emma and her brother Alex play frog toss at the *Harry Potter and the Order of the Phoenix* premiere after-party in 2007. Emma also enjoys field hockey, tennis, and skiing and she is certified to scuba dive.

In an interview with *CosmoGirl*, Emma described herself as both a tomboy and a girly girl. "I can be a bit of a boy when I'm with boys. I also love fashion and makeup. I have fun with my friends choosing clothes and putting nail polish on."

Emma has appeared in magazines around the world. When she was fifteen, she became the youngest person to appear on the cover of *Teen Vogue* magazine.

But she doesn't think of herself as glamorous. "I can be if I want to be. I love dressing up, but it doesn't rule or dictate my life."

In April 2009, Emma **celebrated** (SEH-luh-bray-ted) her nineteenth birthday. "It looks like my birthday has snuck up on me," she wrote on her blog. "I sooo don't want to be 19. I can't believe how much has happened."

Emma was growing up. She had her own car—a Toyota Prius. She had moved out of her parents' home and into her own apartment near Leavesden, where the movie studios are. She was filming the final Harry Potter movies. And she had a boyfriend named Jay Barrymore—although she refused to talk about him publicly.

As she was taking a year off from school, she told *Interview* that she missed it. "I miss the smell of books. I miss my pencil case and ring binders. I want it all back."

She decided to begin a new life in college—in the United States.

Emma models clothes from her People Tree, Love From Emma
clothing collection. She admits she enjoys dressing up sometimes
but is just as happy being a tomboy.

Off to College

In September 2009, Emma enrolled at Brown University in Providence, Rhode Island. She was **majoring** (MAY-jur-ing) in English **literature** (LIH-tur-ih-chur). On her web site, she called college "the most amazing time."

Emma said she enjoys blending in with the other students. "I want to do it properly, like everyone else," she told *The Daily Express*.

The **environment** (en-VY-urn-munt) is an important issue to Emma. In 2009 she was asked to be an **ambassador** (am-BAS-uh-dor) for Greenpeace. The goal of Greenpeace is to raise awareness about protecting the environment. And her clothing line with People Tree, an **eco-friendly** (EE-koh-frend-ly) clothing company, came out in February 2010.

"I cannot, not be green," Emma told *The Daily Mail*. "It's something I feel strongly about."

Emma says her friends tease her about being famous, but one of the perks of being a celebrity is travel. She and Potter costars (left to right) Robbie Coltrane, Matthew Lewis, Oliver Phelps, and James Phelps visited The Wizarding World of Harry Potter in Orlando, Florida, which opened in June 2010.

With so much going on in her life, Emma wishes she had real-life magical powers. "I would love to have a time-turner," she told *Girls' Life*. A time-turner is a kind of time machine from *Prisoner of Azkaban*. "I'm one of these people who tries to fit about 20 million things into my day. And so to be able to rewind time or go forward, that would be ideal."

She admits it's hard leaving Potterworld behind. "It's quite hard to imagine my life without Harry Potter," she said in *The Sunday Observer*. "In a way though I feel it will never be over. The books will always be loved. The films will come on every Christmas. So it'll keep living on in kids' imaginations and adults' imaginations for many years to come."

Emma wants to keep acting, but she believes it will be hard for people to see her in a different role than that of Hermione. She said in *The Daily Telegraph*, "I think it will be hard to pick the next role after this one. I hope I'm talented enough to take on another character."

Whatever Emma puts her mind to, it seems to happen—as if by magic.

CHRONOLOGY

1990 Emma Charlotte Duerre Watson is born on April 15 in Paris, France.

1995 She, her brother, and her mother move to Oxford, England, after her parents divorce.

1998 She enters the Dragon School in Oxford.

1999 Emma auditions for the part of Hermione Granger in *Harry Potter and the Sorcerer's Stone*.

2001 She continues playing the role of Hermione in *Harry Potter and the Chamber of Secrets*.

2003 She graduates from the Dragon School and enters the all-girls Headington School. Meanwhile, she continues to act in the Harry Potter movies.

2004 She appears in *Harry Potter and the Prisoner of Azkaban*.

2005 She appears in *Harry Potter and the Goblet of Fire*.

2007 She appears in *Harry Potter and the Order of the Phoenix* and in the British TV movie *Ballet Shoes* as Pauline Fossil.

2008 She is the voice of Princess Pea in *The Tale of Despereaux*. She begins dating Jay Barrymore.

2009 Emma enters Brown University in Providence, Rhode Island, to study English literature. She appears in *Harry Potter and the Half-Blood Prince*.

2010 In June, she finishes filming the last Harry Potter movie, *Harry Potter and the Deathly Hallows*. It will be released in two parts: one in 2010 and the other in 2011.

FILMOGRAPHY

2011 *Harry Potter and the Deathly Hallows: Part II*

2010 *Harry Potter and the Deathly Hallows: Part I*

2009 *Harry Potter and the Half-Blood Prince*

2008 *The Tale of Despereaux* (voice)

2007 *Harry Potter and the Order of the Phoenix*
Ballet Shoes (TV)
2005 *Harry Potter and the Goblet of Fire*
2004 *Harry Potter and the Prisoner of Azkaban*
2002 *Harry Potter and the Chamber of Secrets*
2001 *Harry Potter and the Sorcerer's Stone*

FIND OUT MORE

Books
Bankston, John. *Daniel Radcliffe*. Hockessin, DE: Mitchell Lane Publishers, 2004, 2010.
Gaines, Ann Graham. *J.K. Rowling*. Hockessin, DE: Mitchell Lane Publishers, 2005, 2007.
Tieck, Sarah. *Emma Watson: Harry Potter Star*. Pinehurst, NC: Buddy Books, 2010.

Works Consulted
Blasberg, Derek. "Emma Watson." *Interview*, May 1, 2009.
Bryson, Jodi. "Emma . . . Hermione . . . Same Girl?" *Girls' Life*, December 1, 2005.
Chang, Rachel. "Three Minutes with Emma Watson." *CosmoGirl,* August 1, 2007.
Clott, Alicia. "Emma Watson." *Girls' Life*, October 1, 2002.
"Desperate Watson 'Pounced' on Grint to Finish Kissing Scene in Harry Potter Flick." *Asian News International*, July 4, 2009. http://www.thaindian.com/ newsportal/entertainment/desperate-watson-pounced-on-grint-to-finish-kissing-scene-in-harry-potter-flick_100213396.html
Ditzian, Eric. "Harry Potter Star Emma Watson on 'Awkward' Kiss with Rupert Grint." *MTV.com*, July 13, 2009. http://www.mtv.com/movies/news/ articles/1615730/story.jhtml
"Emma Watson Has a New Fashion Line." *The Insider*, n.d. http://www. theinsider.com/news/2872166_Emma_Watson_Has_A_New_Fashion_ Line
Hiscock, John. "Interview: Wild About Harry; Emma Watson Loves Working with Potter Co-star Daniel Radcliffe." *The [London] Mirror*, July 13, 2007.
"A Life After Harry Potter." *The Sydney Morning Herald*, July 2, 2007. http://www.smh.com.au/news/film/a-life-after-harry-potter/2007/07/ 01/1183228944244.html

FIND OUT MORE

"Movies & TV: Emma Watson." *New York Times*, n.d. http://movies.nytimes.com/person/300014/Emma-Watson/biography

Pearlman, Cindy. "Potter Stars Just Average Kids." *Post-Tribune*, November 18, 2001.

"Watson and Grint Giggled Through Kiss." *ContactMusic.com*, July 8, 2009. http://www.contactmusic.com/news.nsf/story/watson-and-grint-giggled-through-kiss_1109118

White, Kelly. "Bewitched: Emma Has Us Completely Mesmerized." *Girls' Life*, August 1, 2007.

On the Internet

Emma Watson's Official Web Site
http://www.emmawatsonofficial.com/

Harry Potter Official Web Site
http://harrypotter.warnerbros.com/intro.html

J.K. Rowling Official Web Site
http://www.jkrowling.com/

People Tree: Emma Watson Collection
http://www.peopletree.co.uk/category/emma-watson/

People Tree, Love from Emma
http://peopletree.co.uk/press/sesp_news.php

GLOSSARY

ambassador (am-BAS-uh-dor)—A person who speaks and volunteers for an organization.

attorney (uh-TUR-nee)—Lawyer.

audition (aw-DIH-shun)—A tryout, usually for a part in a play or movie.

boarding school (BOR-ding skool)—A school where students live during the school year.

competition (kom-peh-TIH-shun)—An event in which two or more opposing sides try to win a challenge.

eco-friendly (EE-koh-frend-ly)—Not harmful to the environment and things living in it.

environment (en-VY-urn-munt)—The natural surroundings of living things.

literature (LIH-tur-ih-chur)—Body of written works of a language, period, or culture.

majoring (MAY-jur-ing)—Studying one particular subject for several years, usually at a university.

muggle (MUH-gul)—In Harry Potter, a mean name to call someone whose parents are a wizard or witch and a human.

maternal (muh-TER-nal)—From the mother's side.

overachiever (oh-ver-uh-CHEE-ver)—A person who does above and beyond what is expected of them.

Quidditch (KWIH-ditch)—A game from Harry Potter that involves four balls and players riding broomsticks.

self-conscious (self-KON-shus)—Highly aware of one's own being, actions, or thoughts.

INDEX